Now Faith

Now Faith

CHERYL STASINOWSKY

WORD SCRIBE

Now Faith
Copyright © 2011 by Cheryl Stasinowsky

All rights reserved. No part of this book may be reproduced, stored in a retrieval system, or transmitted in any form or by any means-electronic, mechanical, photocopy, recording, or otherwise-without prior written permission of the copyright owner, except by a reviewer who wishes to quote brief passages in connection with a review for inclusion in a magazine, website, newspaper, podcast, or broadcast.

All Scripture quotations, unless otherwise indicated, are taken from the New King James Version of the Bible. Copyright © 1982 by Thomas Nelson, Inc. Used by permission. All rights reserved.

ISBN: 978-0615899077

Library of Congress Control Number: 2011931936

Take note that the name satan and related names are not capitalized.

Dedication

I dedicate this book to my children, their children, and to the generations that I will never have an opportunity to personally speak to. I am writing this book with you in my heart. I hand you my faith and bless you on your own personal journey of faith with your Lord and Savior Jesus Christ. I love you and am praying for you right now, as I am alive…

This book is written with the purpose of changing the faith of nations, one person at a time.

You are next!

May this book enrich, enhance, and strengthen your personal faith continuously ...

My Family

Acknowledgements

Father, Son, and Holy Spirit, thank You all so much for Your daily moment by moment guidance in my life. I love You and choose every moment to trust You with all of my life. I trust that You know what You are doing even when I do not. I love You!

To my husband, Wally, you are so amazing and I thank you for being my biggest support through my daily pursuit in writing this book. You at times believed more in me and my writing than I did. Thank you and I love you. You are a wonderful husband and father to our children. Yeah for us!

To my children, Amber and Jordan, my heart is so big for the two of you and I love you individually for who you are and who you are becoming. I pray for you every day and night and want all of God's best for you and your futures. May you always find Jesus as your best friend and the Holy Spirit as your comforter and Father God as the one true and holy God to be trusted always. I love you!

To my family and friends, thank you for your prayers, encouraging words, and for believing in me through everything. You are all necessary in my life and I love you!

Contents

Foreword	13
Introduction	15
Hebrews 11	23
11:1	29
We Understand	33
Abel	37
Enoch	43
Noah	49
Abraham	53
Sarah	57
These All Died in Faith	61
Testing of Faith	65
Generational Faith	69
Moses - Destiny Faith	73
Walls of Jericho Fell	77
Rahab	81
And What More Shall I Say?	85
Reflection of Faith	89
About the Author	91

Foreword

Cheryl Stasinowsky takes you on an extremely personal journey. It is as though Cheryl and the great champions of faith, in Hebrews chapter 11, are walking along together with you on a path of shared insights that arrive at practical applications concerning the various aspects of faith. It is so important for people to grasp that between the "substance" of things hoped for, and the "evidence" of things not seen there is a process developing that changes the person before it changes the places. One of the observations Cheryl shares is; "You cannot see faith, but the substance is surrounding Him (God). Faith is a journey of learning, experiencing, receiving, giving and believing in God." This among many other principles are gems that come from a woman of God who has been on a journey of processed wisdom for a long time. Cheryl goes on to challenge the reader to journal their thoughts and she prays confirmational resolve after each chapter to seal the Word shared. I recommend this book to all who hunger to walk on a rich path of cultivated faith with the champions of Hebrews chapter 11 and revelation shared by Cheryl Stasinowsky.

Dr. Rick Kendall
President/ Founder of Global Embassy Network and Victory Ministries Inc. www.globalembassynetwork.com

Introduction

"My brethren, count it all joy when you fall into various trials, knowing that the testing of your faith produces patience" (James 1:2-3). Although this book is on Hebrews 11, my journey through writing this book is connected to this verse. This book was definitely a testing of my faith as I was writing it. Here is a bit of my journey through the test of faith.

When I first began writing, it was such a wonderful journey and it felt so free. I would experience the total inspiration of the Lord each time I wrote and I looked forward to those moments. I learned to process my journey with the Lord and His Word and then share it with others. That is what is contained within my first book, His Hidden Treasures. I wrote on my blog only to help others and never with the intent that it would be a book.

He then opened another desire of my heart to encourage others each day with a relevant word and hence the journey on facebook and my second book, Deeper Relevance. These writings were totally different from what I had ever written prior. They were short and had questions that were intended to stir the reader to connect to the Word with their own life and allow it to process their thoughts. This transition was difficult at the beginning but it soon became normal.

Both of the books published to date were not intended to be a book by me—by the Lord, yes, but I did not see it. This book you are holding is the first I have written with the knowledge of it actually being a book. I know the book inside and out, I have taught it many times and have been living and breathing it for over ten months, since the opening of the revelation on July 29 (in my second book Deeper Relevance), and yet, as I tried to write it in a book, I found it very difficult. I was pressing into the Lord to get this book out of me.

At the beginning, I spent nearly three hours in the prayer house focusing on penning one chapter. I have never experienced this in writing. I realized that He was changing my style yet again and my mind seemed to be resisting a bit. I literally fought giving up and stopped for the day continuously. I finally did get a chapter written. This book is coming from a different place within me. It is not the wonderfully inspired free place that I have always written from which made it feel more like work or exercising. I believe He taught me something totally new.

I knew that I was to write this book on faith (Hebrews 11) and I knew that it was to come out on 11.11.11. It is interesting that I am not writing out of a place of emotion and feelings as I have in the past. As I look at this, I can see that faith, in itself, is not about how we feel and so I am experiencing the very perseverance of faith as I am writing. Our emotions do not establish our faith. Sometimes we feel so wonderful and close to God and other times, we find ourselves questioning and doubting our faith. I think that it makes perfect sense now why

Introduction

I had to push through so very hard to write this book on faith. I know that it carries within it an impartation of faith that is vital to each of us.

He is deepening yet another place within me as He does with each of us. Do we just get comfortable with how we have done things in the past? I am submitted to the struggle and journey of this book. Hebrews 11:1 says, "Now faith is the substance of things hoped for, the evidence of things not seen." This is exactly what this book is about. I am writing about the evidence of the faith of the men and women of God that have gone before us that are not seen. We are each connected to their faith and we have proof of that with verse 40 in chapter 11, "God having provided something better for us, that they should not be made perfect apart from us." This book is about standing before each of these men and women and receiving an impartation of their overcoming faith that is for us…

We each need their faith. I encourage you to read each chapter as many times as you need to and pray the prayer at the end as many times as you desire. Your faith will connect to their faith and you will walk in greater purpose.

I personally have found Hebrews 11 to be a very special chapter in the Bible. It is written like no other chapter in His Word. Below is what created the inspiration for this book:

Fire Tunnel of Faith[1]

"'Now faith is the substance of things hoped for, the evidence of things not seen' (Hebrews 11:1). This is the sign over the "fire tunnel" today; I encourage you to prepare yourself for an

impartation of faith. I see Hebrews chapter 11 as two rows of people filled with faith who believed for the impossible and the writer of Hebrews has positioned us in the front of the line today. You get a private walk through, without all the hurry of hundreds of people before you and behind you. Take as long as you like with each person. Are you ready? Can you see it?

As you get to each person, think about their life. What does He want you to see about them today, for you? Evaluate their faith, and their choices. Look at how He saw them, and then receive their testimony. With each step through today, there is a deposit of faith available. Allow them to touch you and minister to you. As you take the first step, you encounter the world around you and the words that God spoke to create them. Do not move too fast through that one. He has spoken words over you that are still to come, receive the impartation!

As you approach Abel, what do you need? Ponder his life and his death. Is the life and faith of Abel speaking to you? Next step is Enoch who walked so closely with God that he did not die on this earth. What would that life have looked like? His testimony is that he pleased God. Do you need this faith today? You are standing right in front of Enoch; allow him to lay hands on you. If you are still able to walk, you will see another sign in the fire

---

1. A fire tunnel is where you have two lines of spiritual leaders such as pastors, special guests, and prayer team members. Everyone else lines up and walks between the two lines to be prayed for and have the spiritual leaders lay their hands on them for an impartation of the Spirit of God.

Introduction

tunnel today telling us that it is impossible to please God without faith. Good thing we are walking through this fire tunnel of faith today.

What do you need from Noah? Ponder being the only man and family saved from total destruction. Does it at times feel as if the world around us is falling apart? We sure need some of his faith. As you meditate on his life and testimony, receive the faith and courage that Noah had. Are you ready? You are now approaching Abraham. Ponder his life; there is not just one verse about him. Stop for a while at Abraham my friends and receive ...

Next is Sarah and for those of you seeing 11:11 these days, this one might be a good place to camp for a while. Ponder receiving strength to conceive seed. Could the seed be prophetic words, dreams, and ministries? What is He depositing in you? Do you think you are too old? She was past the age, but it was not about her. I repeat, it was not about her. She judged Him faithful who had promised. Be strengthened today to conceive, to believe, to birth, and receive her testimony, I am!

As you pass by each one today, see the message and testimony that is contained within them and take it for you. Do not hurry, no one is waiting to lock the doors or turn out the lights. No one is waiting for you so they can go home. Take all the time you need and be empowered today as you walk through the intoxicating strength of those who had the faith that pleased God. It is for you and me to be encouraged and to continue. See you at the other end!" (Quote from Deeper Relevance by Cheryl Stasinowsky page 220)

That is where it was birthed and I soon found Hebrews 11 to be a common camping ground when my faith within was being beaten up, questioned, feeling defeated, or when I just did not know who I was or where I was going. I would crawl into Hebrews 11 and read it until I felt my faith rise back up within me. Sometimes it would take until the very last verse.

This book is my personal journey with each of these men and women of God and their faith. I pull out of the words on the page a person facing the same struggles of life that we do today and I connect to their faith in God to help me keep going. I hope that as you read, you too will see different aspects of their lives that you need for your journey. I have made this book short and small so that you can keep it with you all the time. There are so many times in our lives that we find ourselves waiting for someone or for an appointment. Those moments are great opportunities to increase your faith right in the wait.

I completely believe that there is an impartation of faith available repeatedly from each of these men and women listed. Maybe you will add to the list as you encounter stories from His Word that minister to you, such as Ruth, Esther, Paul, or any of the many men and women in the Word. Maybe I will write other additions to this book, but for now, I'll start with the main course. Be prepared to have greater courage and faith.

"And they overcame him by the blood of the Lamb and by the word of their testimony, and they did not love their lives to the death" (Revelation 12:11).

Introduction

Each "By faith" statement is a key to opening the door to the testimony to overcoming faith.

Hebrews 11

By Faith We Understand

1 Now faith is the substance of things hoped for, the evidence of things not seen.

2 For by it the elders obtained a good testimony.

3 By faith we understand that the worlds were framed by the Word of God, so that the things which are seen were not made of things which are visible.

Faith at the Dawn of History

4 By faith Abel offered to God a more excellent sacrifice than Cain, through which he obtained witness that he was righteous, God testifying of his gifts; and through it he being dead still speaks.

5 By faith Enoch was taken away so that he did not see death, "and was not found, because God had taken him"; for before he was taken he had this testimony, that he pleased God.

6 But without faith it is impossible to please Him, for he who comes to God must believe that He is, and that He is a rewarder of those who diligently seek Him.

7 By faith Noah, being divinely warned of things not yet seen, moved with godly fear, prepared an ark for the saving of his household, by which he condemned the world and became heir of the righteousness which is according to faith.

Faithful Abraham

8 By faith Abraham obeyed when he was called to go out to the place which he would receive as an inheritance. And he went out, not knowing where he was going.

9 By faith he dwelt in the land of promise as in a foreign country, dwelling in tents with Isaac and Jacob, the heirs with him of the same promise,

10 for he waited for the city which has foundations, whose builder and maker is God.

11 By faith Sarah herself also received strength to conceive seed, and she bore a child when she was past the age, because she judged Him faithful who had promised.

12 Therefore from one man, and him as good as dead, were born as many as the stars of the sky in multitude—innumerable as the sand which is by the seashore.

The Heavenly Hope

13 These all died in faith, not having received the promises, but having seen them afar off were assured of them, embraced them and confessed that they were strangers and pilgrims on the earth.

14 For those who say such things declare plainly that they seek a homeland,

15 And truly if they had called to mind that country from which they had come out, they would have had opportunity to return.

16 But now they desire a better, that is, a heavenly country. Therefore God is not ashamed to be called their God, for He has prepared a city for them.

The Faith of the Patriarchs

17 By faith Abraham, when he was tested, offered up Isaac, and he who had received the promises offered up his only begotten son,

18 of whom it was said, "In Isaac your seed shall be called,"

19 concluding that God was able to raise him up, even from the dead, from which he also received him in a figurative sense.

20 By faith Isaac blessed Jacob and Esau concerning things to come.

21 By faith Jacob, when he was dying, blessed each of the sons of Joseph, and worshiped, leaning on the top of his staff.

22 By faith Joseph, when he was dying, made mention of the departure of the children of Israel, and gave instructions concerning his bones.

The Faith of Moses

23 By faith Moses, when he was born, was hidden three months by his parents, because they saw he was a beautiful child; and they were not afraid of the king's command.

24 By faith Moses, when he became of age, refused to be called the son of Pharaoh's daughter,

25 choosing rather to suffer affliction with the people of God than to enjoy the passing pleasures of sin,

26 esteeming the reproach of Christ greater riches than the treasures in Egypt; for he looked to the reward.

27 By faith he forsook Egypt, not fearing the wrath of the king; for he endured as seeing Him who is invisible.

28 By faith he kept the Passover and the sprinkling of blood, lest he who destroyed the firstborn should touch them.

29 By faith they passed through the Red Sea as by dry land, whereas the Egyptians, attempting to do so, were drowned.

By Faith They Overcame

30 By faith the walls of Jericho fell down after they were encircled for seven days.

31 By faith the harlot Rahab did not perish with those who did not believe, when she had received the spies with peace.

32 And what more shall I say? For the time would fail me to tell of Gideon and Barak and Samson and Jephthah, also of David and Samuel and the prophets:

33 who through faith subdued kingdoms, worked righteousness, obtained promises, stopped the mouths of lions,

34 quenched the violence of fire, escaped the edge of the sword, out of weakness were made strong, became valiant in battle, turned to flight the armies of the aliens.

35 Women received their dead raised to life again. Others were tortured, not accepting deliverance, that they might obtain a better resurrection.

36 Still others had trial of mockings and scourgings, yes, and of chains and imprisonment.

37 They were stoned, they were sawn in two, were tempted, were slain with the sword. They wandered
about in sheepskins and goatskins, being destitute, afflicted, tormented—

38 of whom the world was not worthy. They wandered in deserts and mountains, in dens and caves of the earth.

39 And all these, having obtained a good testimony through faith, did not receive the promise,

40 God having provided something better for us, that they should not be made perfect apart from us.

11:1

"Now faith is the substance of things hoped for, the evidence of things not seen" (Heb. 11:1).

This verse has always challenged me. It at times can seem so very obvious what it means and then other times I feel I have no idea what it really means. It appears that this verse is the definition of faith and is communicating what I can find in the lives of the people that follow. I see it as a thread that is woven into the entire Bible and is what holds it all together.

To open up the mystery of this verse the Lord has taken me on a journey into the word "hope." The word hope makes me think of waiting in expectation or anticipation for something to come. The Lord showed me my hope as a child, as a teen, and finally as an adult. For me personally, my hope changed as my circumstances of life changed. When I was hurt by people, I found that my hope was moved from others to myself. It was a way of protecting me from being hurt again. I recognized that my hope was connected or influenced by disappointments, failures, expectations, and life in general.

I found that where I put my hope was a choice. I put my hope in my gifts and talents, in finances, in my career, and in my own abilities to get things done and keep my life moving forward as I saw it needed to be.

When I met Jesus, everything changed. He began exposing all the places that my hope was not in Him. The tests and trials were His gift to me to connect me closer to Him. Did I see it that way at first? No. Through many struggles and submitting to His plans and purposes, I have begun to see the value in the struggles. As my hope, piece by piece, gets put into Him, there are shifts in the way that I think and go through the process of life that are secure and solid. He taught me about faith through the journey of hope.

I had begun noticing lately that places where I had thought I received a victory in my past were no longer looking like a victory. I had somehow fallen back into the thinking of my past about certain things and people. I had walked through significant reconciliation with people, and yet, lately I found that I was exhibiting an attitude about them once again. As I asked the Lord about it, He showed me Hebrews 11:1.

He showed me that when I personally got the breakthroughs in the relationships, I set up expectations of what I thought the future would be like. I expected them to treat me different and for the relationship to be wonderful. This was the substance of things hoped for. As I journeyed through the days after the reconciliation, I was looking for evidence of a change. I did not do this consciously; I was not aware of my expectations. Those unmet expectations became disappointments. Those disappointments that were not addressed within me turned into unforgiveness, resentment, and bitterness. I had once again put my faith in man in some areas I should not have without realizing it.

I began to forgive the people before the Lord once again and I forgave me. I asked the Lord to forgive them and to forgive me. I wonder how many times we do this. Do you have areas where you have gotten a breakthrough in the past but then started recognizing that you were back to a way of thinking from your past? I want to encourage you to ask the Lord to show you any substance of things that you have hoped for that did not turn out as you expected, allowing disappointment to enter into your thoughts. This influences your faith, relationships, the way you respond to situations, and how you see things in the future.

I now see this as a daily area that I need to address and keep before the Lord to reveal any areas where disappointment has gotten in and started poisoning my faith.

We each have a choice of where we put our faith, hope, and love. Life around us at times can influence our decision without us consciously knowing it. I began this book with this chapter first, because I felt that it might be necessary to ask the Lord to show you any people that you may need to forgive from your past, so that when you are continuing through this book and receiving the impartations of each person of faith, you can receive a greater portion.

Prayer for Preparation

Lord Jesus, I come to You today just as I am. I know that I bring hurts and disappointments from my past. Forgive me for putting my faith, hope, and love in man instead of You. Please show me people that I need to forgive before moving forward in this book. I want to receive the full capacity of faith that each of these men and women who pleased You had. Give me grace and courage to forgive, to be forgiven, and to forgive You. Increase my capacity for more faith so that I can receive overcoming faith as those who have gone before me. Thank You Jesus! Amen.

(I would like to encourage you to take some time with the Lord on this area, prior to moving forward. Remain open throughout this book to the Lord opening areas within you that have hindered you from moving forward. I do firmly believe that each person that I bring before you in this book has something to give you that will change your life.)

We Understand

"By faith we understand that the worlds were framed by the word of God, so that the things which are seen were not made of things which are visible" (Heb. 11:3).

Do we understand this? This really is the beginning of our journey into our faith tunnel and it starts with the Word of God. He did not have to use His hands to create anything in this world, He just had to speak, and everything was framed. Come with me as I attempt to unfold what is available to each of us about what God speaks.

If it has been awhile since you have read about the beginning of the worlds being framed, you might want to pause and go read Genesis chapter 1. As you read it, meditate on the power and completeness of His words. The words that He spoke in the beginning of time that framed the worlds, are still holding their purpose and relevance. What does He want you to see in this verse about Him?

I personally find it interesting that He made everything with His words knowing that scientists would come along trying to prove how everything got here and how old it is. Do we really think that we can fully comprehend and understand such a God who has so much power that He does not have to touch anything? I think He spoke it just to confound the wise and keep man from completely figuring out and rationalizing and justifying the ways of God.

If we put together that we are made in His image, with His spoken words, does He want us to gain understanding of the power of our own words we speak today? When He speaks, He creates. When we speak, we create. We cannot see words, and yet, we can see what is created by them from Him. He gave us an example of the power of words and repeatedly throughout the Word of God; we read about the power of the tongue and see the evidence of it. Do we pay attention to the words we speak or do we just speak what is on our mind and ignore the consequences or hurts that we create by them? Do you need help in this area?

What have you done with words that God has spoken to you? Have you kept them and embraced them or just walked away and quickly forgotten them? Does He want you to place greater value in the words He speaks to you?

Everything in Hebrews chapter 11 connects and flows together. Verse 1 begins by describing what faith is. This chapter then progresses into God Himself speaking words to frame the world that we can only understand by faith. When we get to verse 6, we read that without faith it is impossible to please God. All are connected to verse 3. You cannot see faith but the substance is surrounding Him. Faith is a journey of learning, experiencing, receiving, giving, and believing in God. We can believe that He is and that He is a rewarder of those who diligently seek Him. It takes this faith to begin to understand that the worlds were framed by the Word of God, the unseen breath of God that created what we see around us.

Prayer for Impartaton of Faith

Lord Jesus, Father God, and Holy Spirit, of whom I have been made in Your image, please impart in me a greater faith to believe. Please increase my faith to displace all the doubts and fears that are within me, known and unknown. Please impart in me a greater understanding and self-control of the words that I speak on a daily basis. May I be a person of few words and great wisdom. Help me to hold closely and value greatly words that You speak to me. Lord, I believe but please help my unbelief in all areas of my faith. Deepen my faith and awaken a fresh desire to please You and diligently seek You in all things. Please Holy Spirit help me every moment of the day and in every situation to choose my words carefully knowing that they have power to bring life and power to bring death. Please impart in me a greater understanding of the faith that pleases You. You are so wise, so loving and caring, so complete and perfect in every way, please impart in me a greater portion of faith. Thank You for leading the way as a great example and for creating me for such a time as this. I ask all this in the name of Jesus, amen!

Abel

"By faith Abel offered to God a more excellent sacrifice than Cain, through which he obtained witness that he was righteous, God testifying of his gifts; and through it he being dead still speaks" (Heb. 11:4).

We have opened the door to the life and faith of Abel. Come with me as we unlock and receive an impartation from his life that God is testifying of.

In Genesis 4:2-10, we can read that Abel was the second born to Adam and Eve. He was a keeper of the sheep and his older brother Cain was a tiller of the ground. Abel and Cain both brought an offering to the Lord, and yet, they were not received the same. The Lord respected Abel and his offering and He did not respect the offering of Cain. As the story goes on in Genesis, Cain ends up killing Abel in the field. As we look at these few verses of Abel what can we see about his life?

We can first look at the relationship of the family. Cain became jealous of his brother. Do we as parents show partiality to one child over another? Did Adam and Eve do this with their boys? We know that God did, so there is something in the stewarding of the favor of another that we can learn to walk in. As I look within me, I see times when I have not felt that something was fair in how a situation was handled. How do you handle situations when someone else is looked at as better than you? Or promoted over you and you did not feel they were as qualified as you are? God knew what was happening and tried to warn Cain in verse 7, "If you do well, will you not be accepted? And if you do not do well, sin lies at the door.

And its desire is for you, but you should rule over it." God is telling Cain and us that we can rule over sin. We can rule over the feelings and thoughts of jealousy that want to arise when we find ourselves in these situations. If this is an area where you have struggled, and have not ruled over it as well as you should have, you can repent and ask the Lord to help you right now. I am going to continue, but you can stay here as long as you like.

Abel is a keeper of the sheep. I see a connection here with Abel and the life of King David who was a shepherd boy. His faith grew as he kept the sheep of his father and fought off the enemies that came to attack the sheep. David's life as a shepherd prepared him. I personally think that the life of a shepherd is quiet and you would have time to think and talk to the Lord. Cain was a tiller of the ground and we know that the ground was cursed in Genesis 3:17c. Did the hardship of his occupation influence how he saw things?

Abel

I think of the world around us today and the demands and pressures to do better, work harder, and faster. We find ourselves in a technologically-driven world that is influenced by a constant sense of urgency. I remember life before cell phones and computers. I remember life before the internet. I see so many things in the world around us pulling at our time. I think Cain allowed the hard labor to influence how he saw what his brother was doing. While he was pounding on the ground, did he look over and see his brother lying under a tree resting? I think this stirred up jealousy. I think this created an issue within Cain, making him feel he worked harder but at the same time, did not see that he was not really giving the best of what he had to God. Do we do this? Allow the Lord to reveal any truth to you that might be hidden within your heart and that is influencing how you perceive others and what you might be giving to God.

I see that Abel gave from his heart and Cain gave out of obligation. If we toil or strive to get somewhere or accomplish something that possibly God is not on, then this influences where we are giving from. I have to wonder if this is a breeding ground for entitlement. Do we feel we are entitled to something because we have worked so hard? Where are you within the influences of the situations that you encounter and that you see happening with others around you?

I find it interesting that Abel did not follow in the footsteps of his older brother. Abel was somehow able to gain respect from God. Abel was able. The faith of Abel that is available to us in this moment enables us to gain respect from God. We are responsible for how we live our lives each day. We are each given the same amount of time. The enemy loves us to blame others and to follow others down paths that are not meant for us. Abel did not follow the example of his brother. Abel had his eyes and heart connected to God.

God respected Abel's offering over that of Cain. I personally have been learning how to give an offering to the Lord as people praise me for what I have done. I receive the praise from man and then quickly run to the Lord to give it to Him. I am still learning this, but I do see that Abel gave out of his relationship with God and we can too. Do you think about giving an offering to the Lord that is not just financial? What area is the Lord showing you that can enhance what you give to the Lord?

Every day of our lives, we encounter one of the areas contained within the testimony of Abel, whether it is in our families, our work places, or our relationships with others. I pray that today you will have a greater awareness and understanding of how you are being influenced and you will seek the Lord for His wisdom and direction in all.

Prayer for Impartation of Faith

Oh Lord Jesus, as I stand before You and Abel and all that is contained within the testimony of his life that pleased You, I ask for an impartation of the faith that Abel had that caused You to testify of him. I do not want to be influenced by the world around me, but only by You. Help me to not get caught up by the jealousy of others. Help me to stay focused on You as Abel did. I need enabling faith. In whatever situation that I find myself in today and each day, may the faith of

Abel

Abel grow within me more and more. Impart in me the understanding of giving out of my relationship with You. I desire a testimony that speaks even after I am dead. Please impart the faith that I need to walk in this. Thank You for the testimony of Abel and for the changes that are now going to take place within me from his life and Your influence in mine. In Jesus' name, amen!

Enoch

"By faith Enoch was taken away so that he did not see death, 'and was not found, because God had taken him'; for before he was taken he had this testinmony, that he pleased God" (Heb. 11:5).

We stand before Enoch today and the faith that was contained within him. As you stand there, what would you ask him? What is it about the life of Enoch that you want to receive?

Just as we did not know much about the life of Abel, with Enoch, we know even less, but he pleased God. If we go back to Genesis 5 where we are first introduced to Enoch, we will see his name in the family of Adam. Enoch was in the seventh generation of man and he walked with God for 300 years. Allow your mind and heart to connect with such a relationship. As you stand before Enoch today, this part of his testimony is available to you.

I cannot help but wonder what it would have looked like and been like to walk with God for 300 years. I personally received Jesus as my Savior when I was seventeen and now I am almost fifty. The last nine years I have been on a journey of walking with God, as I perceive Enoch did. We do not even live that long anymore. If we look a little closer, we will see that Enoch died at age 365 (there are 365 days in a year) and he walked with God 300 years, so what happened to him at age 65? Many of us struggle with believing the lies that we are too old to get it or too old to start. If this is you, allow the Lord to deposit truth within you today as you connect with the fact that at the age of 65 Enoch began his close relationship with God. It is not too late to start.

I think of what a daily walk with God would be like. Think about it, it would influence everything within you. Walking with God would communicate a closeness and conversation. Enoch knew and pleased God. I would have loved to have heard their conversations. I think of the influence on Enoch's thoughts, his words, and his perspective of things around him that this relationship would have had. Everything was affected by his relationship with God. We know that God is love (1 John 4:8). Enoch was in a relationship and walked with love. Do you want this? Is this what you desire to connect to as you stand before Enoch?

As we look at the times that Enoch walked in, we can see that the people were evil and see in Genesis 6:6 that the Lord was sorry that He had made man on the earth. I would think that we can surmise that Enoch was not sheltered from this. As he walked with God, he also walked with the people in the world around him, as we do. We do not read about the Lord protecting him or rescuing him. We do not read about people knocking at the door trying to harm him (Lot). We do not read about the Lord sending him to proclaim judgment on people (Jonah). How is the world around you today influencing or affecting you? Do you see the world around you today as evil? Are you possibly blaming your circumstances for a lack of relationship with God? What is it that you need from the faith of Enoch today? Receive it…

Look at the generational line of Enoch. His great grandson was Noah. What did Enoch pass down to the generations? We do not know what he did or did not pass down as we do with King David and Solomon, his son. So is that which is within the generations of Enoch for us today? We can look at our life and give to the next generation. There are people around us observing us by our words, our actions, and our responses. What did the children of Enoch see in his relationship with God? Enoch had sons and daughters, but only the line that came from his son, Methuselah, endured through the flood (Genesis 5:27-29). Just a fun fact, Methuselah lived the longest of any man—969 years. Was this length of life in any way connected to Enoch's relationship with God? You would think that Enoch would have spoken with all of his children about his relationship with God. Why did some not make it through the flood? Have you ever noticed that? If you need an impartation from the faith of Enoch to give to future generations, then receive…

In the verse above, we see that Enoch had a testimony. His testimony was that he pleased God. We can please God. How do we please a God that is all knowing, all wise, perfect, complete, and lacking nothing? Before we get totally discouraged by such an impossible thought, we have to go to

Mark 10:27, "But Jesus looked at them and said, 'With men it is impossible, but not with God; for with God all things are possible.'" Enoch walked with God. Enoch pleased God. If we continue on to the next verse in Hebrews, we will read a powerful statement that is connected to Enoch, "But without faith it is impossible to please Him, for he who comes to God must believe that He is, and that He is a rewarder of those who diligently seek Him." By his faith, Enoch pleased God. Enoch came to God and believed. How do we know that he believed? He walked with God for 300 years. Enoch knew God and believed in who He was. Do you need this from Enoch? Allow the Lord to give you an impartation of the faith of Enoch.

As I was writing this chapter, I went for a walk with the life of Enoch in mind. I thought of all the many ways that God speaks to me through His Creation, His Word, through songs, people, and anything and everything around me. As I began looking at His Creation and praising God for the beauty of it, I realized I was walking with God. Maybe not at the same level or capacity as Enoch, but for the moment that I was in, I was walking with God. Walking with God as Enoch did is walking with an awareness of God being with you every moment that you are here on this earth. We can walk with Him and talk with Him all the time as He is always there for us.

PRAYER FOR IMPARTATION OF FAITH

Oh Lord Jesus, today I stand before You and remember Enoch. I ask that You would give me the relationship that Enoch had with You. I want to walk with You every moment of the day and night. I want to think as You think and speak as You speak. Help me to walk and love as You do. Please impart in me the faith of Enoch that pleased You. I want to come to You and believe that You are and that You are a rewarder of those who diligently seek You. Renew my diligence and help my unbelief. I trust that You have heard my prayer and that impartation is already beginning. Give me the courage and wisdom to walk this out. Thank You for all that You are doing and are going to do within me. May it be said of me that I pleased God and walked with God all the days of my life. In Jesus' name, amen!

Noah

"By faith Noah, being divinely warned of things not yet seen, moved with godly fear, prepared an ark for the saving of his household, by which he condemned the world and became heir of the righteousness which is according to faith" (Heb. 11:7).

Noah is one of my heroes. I cannot even begin to imagine what this warning must have looked like to take on a task as he was asked to do. Come with me as we journey into the life of Noah to gain an understanding of just who it is that we are standing before and whose faith we are receiving an impartation from.

"This is the genealogy of Noah. Noah was a just man, perfect in his generations. Noah walked with God" (Genesis 6:9). Noah too walked with God as his great grandfather Enoch. Noah began his life living in the same corruption that Enoch did, and yet, he was able to walk with God through it. As I meditate on this "walked with God" statement, I am focused on the word "with." Both Enoch and Noah walked with God. In Mark 10:27 we read, "But Jesus looked at them and said, 'With men it is impossible, but not with God; for with God all things are possible.'" Do we recognize who we keep company with? Do our words attract the wrong company? Just a thought to ponder and examine within…

What must it have been like to walk with God so closely that Noah's was the only family to be chosen to live and everyone else around him destroyed? God was not happy with how His creation had turned out and was starting over. He could have just destroyed everyone and everything and none of us would have ever known the difference. He could have easily started over with man, but there was something about Noah and the relationship that he and God had that made God spare him. He instructed Noah to build a boat in the midst of this corruption. This task brought attention to Noah and with it more persecution; and yet, Noah continued with what God asked him to do. In his daily walk with God, he had stepped into the possible with God that Jesus talked about. He was focused, purposed, and built that enormous boat knowing what was coming. To those of us who have read the story, we know what is going to happen and we clearly understand what rain like that can do. But it had never rained on the earth before, so a boat being built that large on land would have been ridiculous in the eyes of man. Noah walked in the possible of God and not man.

These two men stepped into the possible with God because of their relationship with God. This should encourage us. When things are looking impossible around us, we are in the mindset of "with men" and we can become aware of it and repent. The relationship that Enoch and Noah had with God is also available to us "with God." We can walk with God to the unlimited extent of believing that all things are possible, and everything that we approach and encounter is addressed with that focus and awareness. May all of our mindsets shift into this way of thinking. May each of us have a greater desire to purpose and to walk with God. Our circumstances expose the areas that have not yet fully received the revelation of this when we are overwhelmed with life or fearing what we are facing. Consider them all joy because these areas too, are encountering the possibility of receiving a life changing revelation.

Have you been asked by God to do something beyond what you have ever seen? Noah understands hard, difficult, persecution, mocking, being misunderstood, and being made fun of. Noah understands what it means to be focused only on what the Lord has given him to do for many years (it took 75-100 years to build the ark). I wonder what he would have been thinking every day, as he would get up to begin building again. Did he ever doubt that this big flood would come? Did the voices of the people around him disturb his focus or thinking? God asked him to do something that was very public and he could not hide at all what he was doing. We hear nothing about his wife and children until they all get in the ark— did they help? I wonder if Noah ever felt alone. I admire his obedience, faith, and perseverance. We know from the verse prior that Noah's faith pleased God. God was so pleased with Noah that He saved his family and continued creation from his family line. What do you need from the faith and life of Noah?

Now Faith

Prayer for Impartation of Faith

Oh Lord Jesus, I deeply need the courage, focus, and obedience that Noah had. I desire an impartation of his faith that pleased You. I need faith that can stand against all opposition and persecution. Please deposit within me today visions and dreams again that are from You and the faith to walk them out. Please position me with others that will encourage and help me to learn this. I need this faith that Noah had so that I can give it to the generations to come. I want to walk with You as Noah did and look at every situation as possible. I choose today to receive what I need from You from the faith and life of Noah. Thank You for my future with You and all the amazing things I get to do with You by my side. I love You! In Jesus' name, amen.

Abraham

"By faith Abraham obeyed when he was called to go out to the place which he would receive as an inheritance. And he went out, not knowing where he was going" (Heb. 11:8).

Buckle your seat belts for the ride with Abraham. For the first time, we get to truly experience what it looks like to walk with God and to be a friend of God. I would encourage you to read about his life in Genesis chapters 12-25, as that is where we get a picture of his life with God. Abraham alone would be an entire book and so as I stand before him, I will pull out the highlights that the Lord points out to me to open to you. (I would like to suggest listening to these chapters as God tells you a story about His friend.

Abraham is a familiar person in the Bible and we get to see much of his life. As I listened to these chapters in Genesis, I heard God speaking to Abram and giving him instructions. I heard Abram obeying by moving and taking everything he had to a place he did not know. Abram did not follow God's instructions perfectly, and yet, God still worked with him. Abram receives big promises from God as to his future. He rescues Lot, his nephew, and gives the first tithe to Melchizedek. I smile inside as I listen to Abram trying to save his life by not telling the complete truth as he encounters situations with his wife and the people that they encounter as they journey through cities. I hear him reacting to fear. I hear God blessing him through the journey of walking with Him. I hear God continually coming to Abram, His friend, and making a covenant with him, telling him his plans for Sodom and Gomorrah, and casting visions of his inheritance.

I hear Abram questioning the decision that his Friend is making in wanting to destroy two cities. Abram knows that his nephew Lot lives in those cities and approaches God to possibly change His plans. God listens and Lot and his two daughters are spared. Abram receives visitations from God and God continues to work with Abram. Abram receives a name change and finally receives his promised son and steps into all that God has been speaking to him. This took years of conversations, moves, mistakes, and at times getting ahead of the plan of God. Through it all God was faithful and Abraham learned this through the journey with God. God says that it was accounted to him for righteousness and I believe that Abraham would say the same thing about God as we stand before him.

As we learn from Abraham, I believe he would impart to us a relationship with God that we need. He did not walk a perfect path with God. Abraham gives us today a lasting, enduring, and learned obedient faith. It took many years before he received the ultimate promise, and yet, neither

God nor Abraham quit or gave up on each other for it to be fulfilled. It did not matter what Abraham did, God stayed with him through it all and used it for His good. Abraham brings us an impartation with years of experience of coming to God and learning to believe that He is a rewarder of those who diligently seek Him. He was not a perfect man, but he grew and changed through each challenging experience.

Receive what the life of Abraham has to impart to you on your journey with God. What have you done with the promises God has spoken over you? The enemy works so many schemes to try to get us to let go of promises. The days that we live in of instant everything, can influence and affect our patience to wait on God, if we are not careful.

Imagine standing before a man like Abraham with years of experience of pleasing God. I believe he would tell you that when he messed up he had to fight through the wrong decisions just like we do today. Can you feel his compassion for you in his faith? He had a relationship with God as a friend and the friendship grew as he made mistakes just as it can for us. This relationship is not like any that we will experience here on earth and we, at times, place what we have learned with other relationships as how it is with God. Yet, we see the faithful side of God that He wants to give us too. Receive the impartation of the possibility to have a friendship with God that continuously strengthens and gives grace and mercy like you have never experienced. He will rework your mindset on friendships with this impartation. What do you need from the life and faith of Abraham? He wants to give it.

Now Faith

Prayer for Impartation of Faith

Lord Jesus, standing before Abraham is such a privilege and gift. Thank You for allowing me to see what a true friendship with You is like. Change my mindsets in all areas that are not in agreement with how You see me and think of me. You never left Abraham no matter what happened or what mistakes he made. Thank You, that You may also do that for me. Help me in the areas where I have believed a lie that You will not. Please impart to me the experience and learning that Abraham had with You. Help me to wait on You for Your perfect timing of the promises that You have given me. Impart to me a refreshed perspective of You and my family. Impart to me the lasting, enduring, and learned obedient faith that Abraham had. Please forgive me for all the times I have made mistakes and got ahead of You or even lied in the face of fear. I want, desire, and need the faith and relationship that Abraham had with You. I am part of the inheritance that You promised Abraham thousands of years ago, help me to receive and walk in them. Thank You for allowing me to receive from Abraham and for giving me the opportunity to see his life. Thank You for the friendship You are going to teach me to have with You. Thank You that I get to walk with You and talk with You and that You are always with me and for me. I want it to be said of me that it is accounted to me for righteousness. In the name of Jesus, amen.

Sarah

"By faith Sarah herself also received strength to conceive seed, and she bore a child when she was past the age, because she judged Him faithful who had promised" (Heb. 11:11).

As we pass by Sarah, may we go extra slow to pull everything out of her life we need. It is as if we need the ride to stop for awhile and not let it keep going because we do not want to miss anything from her life. Come with me as the ride of faith stops in front of Sarah, Abraham's wife and Isaac's mother.

We find Sarai being mentioned in Genesis chapter 12 while she is traveling with her husband and he asks her to tell a lie so that he will not be killed. We know that she is beautiful. We do not hear her questioning what Abram has told her and she seems to come into agreement with it. God intervenes to save His plans for Sarai and Abram; what did Sarai think when this happened? We then read about Sarai trying to help God and His promise to Abram in Genesis chapter 16. Every time I read this, I cannot believe that she would tell her husband to go into her maid to conceive a child. Does this bother you?

What does this say about how Sarai felt about the promise of God given to her husband? We see that this was not a great plan and that the maid actually then begins thinking she is better than Sarai and parades it in her face. Sarai sends her away. Sarah also gets a name change in Genesis 17:15 and it is as if something shifted. In chapter 18, we observe the prophetic word given to Abraham about Sarah now receiving an appointed time to have a child at the age of 90, well past the childbearing age. Sarah in the tent nearby laughs at such words and is questioned by her response. She lies as to what she did.

When we read about Sarah, we see her as an old woman who lied, gave her husband to another woman to bear a child, laughed at the prophetic word, and then lied again. But if we take a closer look at her, we see a woman who learned through her own life experience and the miracle of bearing a child past her child bearing years, that God is able to do anything. If we were on one of those rides at an amusement park and it was just passing by, we would only be able to focus on this old woman who lied, gave her husband to another woman to have a child, laughed at the prophetic word, and lied yet again. But when we stop the ride and look into the eyes of Sarah, we see a woman who learned through life experience that God is able to do anything He wants. Through the lies, the dreams, the disappointments, the misguided interventions, the failures, struggles, heartache, and even laughter, she witnessed the faithfulness of God in her life.

I cannot help but see the pain that would have been in her eyes as woman after woman became pregnant around her and all the joy that they experienced through the process was before her. Did she dream of the day when it would be her turn? When her turn never came and all of those children around her grew up and had their own children, Sarah was this not disappointment all over again? How did she deal with her self-worth? Did she know that she was receiving strength to conceive seed as she watched her time for such pleasure and satisfaction move past her? Are you observing people around you with their dreams being fulfilled and are you still waiting? Sarah is before you to impart greater faith in the One who promised you such a dream.

All of the experiences of life that were preparing Sarah to conceive seed are before you right now. She learned the faithfulness of God through all of them and when she finally concluded that it was not about her, she conceived. Age does not matter to the Lord. The mistakes that you have made do matter to the Lord, but He forgives you and picks you back up again and places you right where you need to be. If we think that we can mess up God's plans for our lives, then we think of our God as being too small. Sarah offers life experience through disappointments and mistakes. She witnessed God never giving up on her and doing the impossible with her. She fully and completely understands God fulfilling His promises and is indeed a recipient of the reward promised in Hebrews 11:6.

Now Faith

Prayer for Impartation of Faith

Dear Lord Jesus, as I am before Sarah I realize that I definitely need an impartation of her faith. Please deposit in me how she learned about Your faithfulness through all of the challenges of her life. May this enable me to see You through my own struggles and hardships. I need her faith to walk through my own disappointments and heart aches. Forgive me for the times I, too, have lied and tried to help You out with a promise You gave me. Forgive me for thinking You cannot do anything. I want to receive the strength that Sarah had to conceive seed for what is coming and for what You have promised. Help me to rejoice with those around me that walk in the promises that You have given me that have not been realized yet. Impart in me, Almighty God, the faith of Sarah. Thank You for all of the situations and struggles of my life that are teaching and preparing me for Your plans and purposes for my life. Thank You for the life of Sarah and all that is contained in her faith that I am now receiving. I receive her faith, by faith. In Jesus' name, amen!

These All Died in Faith

"These all died in faith, not having received the promises, but having seen them afar off were assured of them, embraced them and confessed that they were strangers and pilgrims on the earth" (Heb. 11:13).

The title over these next four verses in my Bible is "The Heavenly Hope." These verses to me are a transition, but from what? Are they talking about the people written about prior to these verses or the people following these four verses? Does it even matter? Let us approach this verse to be all-inclusive.

We have walked before five people to this point in the book and more are going to follow, so I will not go into their individual lives, but look at a pattern that each of them carried to sustain their faith. Not all of the men and women in Hebrews 11 received their promises, which communicates that their faith was not based on the promise itself. If you focus just on the fact that they did not receive their promises, you could get discouraged, and yet, the promises were generational promises that they were given. Did they realize that? Has the Lord personally given you promises that are beyond you? I wonder how many times someone is given this type of promise and when they get to the end of their life they die feeling that they failed and did not fulfill their promise. What did all of these that died in faith see?

They saw their promises afar off and were assured of them. Was the assurance a continual reminder? We see this clearly in the life of Abraham as the Lord would continually visit him and replay the vision with the stars of the sky and the dust on the earth. The Lord Himself keeps the promise before Abraham; this was his assurance of them. Do you need this?

The Patriarchs embraced these promises. How did they embrace a promise? I see the word embrace here meaning that they held onto the promises. As they looked at choices in their daily life, they would pull out the promise almost as a compass to keep them on that path. They would keep them in their thoughts so that their minds embraced them. They might have had them written down to remind themselves on the challenging days. Do you need this ability?

They confessed that they were strangers and pilgrims on the earth. What does that look like? I believe that their promises had been so assured in them and they embraced them so deeply that they were consumed with moving forward with the promise and agreed with heaven on how that was to be walked out. They came to a point in their walk of faith with

God where He was their reward. Step inside, each of the men and women of faith, and think about what God had asked them to do and the mindset that they would have possessed to walk in such faith. God visited them and a vision and promise grew inside of them and became one with who they had become. They transitioned from being men and women on this earth serving themselves and those around them to serving God in Heaven. Take a moment to look back over each of their lives and you will see this common thread within the verses. They each saw something beyond them and grabbed a hold of it. Is this what you need?

I see each of them as heavenly minded. God wants us to know that there is a relationship available with Him where the struggles of this life do not compare to the promises He has given. He is the heavenly hope and focus that each of them had. He is the reward that each of them received. They were not discouraged that they did not see the promises fulfilled. They handed the vision and promise to the next generation, they took it further, and it kept going and it is now before us.

I believe that what is available to you and me is greater clarity, focus, purpose, and a way to continually embrace the promise while walking on this earth. Are you ready to receive your impartation? Imagine at this moment in time, all of those who died in faith standing around you…

Now Faith

Prayer for Impartation of Faith

Lord Jesus, how I need the faith and vision that all of the men and women had that are contained within Hebrews 11. Please expand my mind and my focus to agree with You. Impart in me the relationship to receive such promises and give me a greater capacity to embrace and confess them. Forgive me for the promises I have received to this point and have let them go or forgot about them. Please hand them to me again and assure me of them as many times as necessary until I am able to carry these visions on my part of the journey. Give me wisdom in what to give to the next generation and may I learn at a greater depth how to keep my hope in heaven and not earth. Please impart in me that ability, I need it so very much. Awaken my purpose again. Awaken my focus on You again. I need greater strength and courage as each of these men and women had. Please impart their collective faith, hope, vision, and assurance within me. Thank You! I ask all of this in the name of Jesus, amen!

Testing of Faith

"By faith Abraham, when he was tested, offered up Isaac, and he who had received the promises offered up his only begotten son" (Heb. 11:17).

This entire situation shakes me up. I know that it was a literal event, and yet, for us today it is symbolic. In this day and age, if we did this literally we would be put in prison, thought of as a fool or crazy person and our child would need counseling for the rest of their life. Come with me as we look into the eyes of Abraham again and see another aspect of his faith that we need today.

In Genesis 22, we find the entire situation that the writer in Hebrews is referencing. I want to draw your attention to a statement in the first verse of this chapter, "Now it came to pass after these things that God tested Abraham." This is after Abraham walked through everything that we have already looked at and now had his promise right in front of him. He had been walking with this promise for some time as the baby grew into a lad and they walked together. This communicates that their bond had grown and Abraham was nurturing and teaching his son about life and his faith. But now it came to pass that this relationship and the promise received needed to be tested. Why? What was Isaac thinking as his dad laid the wood on him and raised a knife? God was watching and looking into the heart of Abraham. When God sees that Abraham's heart is where He needs it to be to fulfill who He has called him to be, God provides the ram instead.

Can you see the picture of this in the eyes of Abraham? What is Abraham speaking to you? Have you received promises and enjoyed them, loved them, and walked with them, but were unable to give them up? I am personally amazed at the obedience and sharpness of hearing God's voice that Abraham displays in this moment. His faith has deepened and we do not see fear anymore. He is sure and is not questioning what God has asked him to do and Abraham is sensitive to a change in direction or instruction at a moment's notice. He does not waiver. He has walked with God through all of the situations of life and his faith has increased. We hear no emotion, crying, or agony of what he is asked to do. He does not even question or have a conversation with God asking Him to change His mind or reminding Him of the promise that God gave him through this child. Do we do this? Isaac represents to us the promises that God has given us. Isaac represents the jobs, the ministries, the homes, the families, the success, and everything else that we have been promised and received. He could also represent blessings in our life.

Testing of Faith

We do get tested in our faith. These tests are not because we are doing something wrong, but because God wants to see how we are stewarding what we have been given. This shows us what is within us. Do we resist or submit? Can we easily let go? In the eyes of Abraham, we see a man who has walked with God and he has learned that his Friend is faithful and can do anything. Through the journey, his trust in God grew. What do you need from Abraham? He is standing before you again to give to you the portion of his faith that you need to grow in the trust and obedience that he had.

Prayer for Impartation of Faith

Lord Jesus, I need an impartation of the faith that Abraham had with You. Please impart in me what is needed to pass the tests of my own personal faith. Enhance my obedience and sensitivity to Your voice. Please deposit within me the unquestionable faith of Abraham. Please impart in me the faith that always passes every necessary test that You deem needed and may my conclusion be that You are able to do anything with the result. Please increase my faith to not doubt or question what You ask me to do. Help me to only rely on You and Your guidance just as Abraham did. He did not ask his friends or go to his pastor, he just obeyed, and he trusted You. I want that faith, God. Increase and impart a deeper level of the faith of Abraham. Thank You for this example to give me understanding in my life today. Thank You for giving meaning to the tests. May I now walk in greater faith to pass the tests that come my way. In Jesus' name, amen!

Generational Faith

As I read Hebrews 11, verses 20 – 22, I see generational faith. I want to encourage you to read these verses and see the handing of the baton from one generation to the next. Do you think generationally? Are there things that you can personally give or leave for the next generation and for the generations to come that you will never see? Within this chapter is an impartation to open generational thinking and strategies, come with me and receive…

In verse 20, we read that by faith Isaac, the promised child of Abraham and Sarah, blesses his two sons. You can view this moment of blessing as a nice way of saying good-bye, or you can see it as imparting faith to the next generation. Think for a moment about all that Isaac has experienced, heard, and seen in his lifetime. Think about the moments that he and his father Abraham had as he was growing up and learning about the God of his father. Isaac was a promised child that carried an inherited promise of God to be the father of many nations.

That prayer over Jacob and Esau was filled with his learned faith in God and in this moment, he gives it to his sons. Do we think this way?

In verse 21, we read that by faith Jacob, when he was dying, blessed each of the sons of Joseph. Jacob received something the day that his father Isaac prayed and blessed him and now it was his moment in time to give to his grandchildren. If you go back to Genesis 49, you will see that Jacob does bless each of his sons, but in Hebrews 11, we see a grandfather blessing his grandchildren. Since the beginning of man, God placed it within us to pass something on to the next generation. Not just a financial inheritance, but the faith that is necessary to walk in greater levels of faith. Why is this necessary? If we do not do this, does something have the potential to get lost? I believe God thinks generationally, so we can too.

What is it within the lines of faith that you can give to the generations that follow you? May a new purpose be awakened within you today for generations that you will never see. In Deuteronomy 6, we see the Lord giving instructions to teach our children about loving the Lord our God with all of our heart, soul, and strength. While we are raising our children, they are witnessing our walk with God and learning what that looks like and feels like. Are we aware of this? When we go to them asking for their forgiveness when we have made a mistake, what are they learning? What is it in our daily life that we can give to them that they will give to their children? Our children and grandchildren are going to give something to theirs, so purpose for them to see a life that loves the Lord in actions, words, thoughts, behavior, and choices. We do not have to wait until we are leaving this world to finally decide to give them our faith. We can model it each day (it is not too late to start) and then when the moment comes to bless our children and grandchildren, we are truly giving them our life experiences and a walk with Jesus and they will understand the weight and responsibility of it and appreciate it even more. Our faith is of great value to the generations that are to come.

Prayer for Impartaion of Faith

Lord Jesus, please awaken in me the heart and mind of the future generations just as Isaac and Jacob did as they blessed their children and grandchildren. Please give me a greater vision and purpose for the generations that follow. Show me what I can give and how I can give it. Forgive me for how I have modeled my faith to this point and help me to walk in new ways with You each day starting now. Give me creative strategies for my family and may I impart generational faith to those that I am responsible for so that they give to those they are responsible for and may the baton of faith in You be handed down and grow as it does. May I have a new heart and mind to care for and steward the faith that I have and live and walk with You in ways that will be spoken about in generations to come. Help me, Jesus, to receive generational faith, as You desire for me to have. I love You and thank You. In Jesus' name, amen!

Moses – Destiny Faith

"By faith Moses, when he was born, was hidden three months by his parents, because they saw he was a beautiful child; and they were not afraid of the king's command" (Heb. 11:23).

For the longest time this verse just seemed out of place and did not fit into the perceived box that I had of the pattern the writer of Hebrews was establishing. How does the decision of his parents get accredited to his faith? How did being beautiful give him faith? Have you ever wondered about that? There are seven verses about the faith of Moses and this got my attention. Come with me, as we look closer to see just what his parents saw.

If you are not familiar with the life of Moses, you might want to take a detour, before reading on, into Exodus 2 to the end of Deuteronomy to gain understanding of his life, and how the Lord used him. As I asked the Lord what was really happening when these parents saw that he was beautiful, He showed me that they saw his destiny. The parents of Moses saw the plans and purposes of the Lord for this young child. When they saw this, courage rose up in them to not be afraid of the king's command.

As you approach each verse of Moses in this chapter you begin to see what they saw unfold. As he grew older, he became more and more aware of his own destiny and faced significant moments in his life where everything changed for him. By his parents positioning him in the beginning and not walking in fear, God rose up a mighty man of God who faced fear like his parents did. In verse 27, we see that Moses, too, did not fear the wrath of the king.

From the faith of Moses, we can receive an impartation to see the destiny of our children and be encouraged to face fears as to the consequences of what that might look like. His parents saw into his future and we too can see into the future of our children, grandchildren, nieces, nephews, and others that the Lord has put in our lives to speak into and be a part of them walking in the fullness of God.

I think from the life and faith of Moses today we receive courage, boldness, favor, destiny, vision, purpose, and an enhanced relationship with God and who He is and what He can do through us. As you position yourself to receive from the faith of such a man, focus on all that he walked through and endured and receive what you specifically need right now in this moment from his life. We see his journey and we are each on a journey. Are you ready?

Moses – Destiny Faith

Prayer for Impartation of Faith

Lord Jesus, as I stand before Moses, I ask for the exact part of his faith and life that I need right now. I ask for the impartation of the faith and vision of his parents to see the destiny of my own children, grandchildren, nieces, nephews, and the lives of the people you have placed around me. Open my eyes to see and may the impartation of courage be within the vision in the name of Jesus. Forgive me for thinking too small about myself and others. Thank You that You have plans and purposes for me and for those around me. Lord Jesus, I want faith that creates destiny. I want to see the destiny, walk in the courage and boldness to get there, and remain focused on Your plans and purposes. Thank You for the life of Moses and his parents and their faith. Thank You for the impartation of destiny faith to give to future generations. Thank You for the direction and answers that I will receive because of this impartation. I receive all of this in the name of Jesus, amen!

Walls of Jericho Fell

"By faith the walls of Jericho fell down after they were encircled for seven days" (Heb. 11:30).

This is an interesting statement. There is not a particular name or person following this "by faith" verse. For the longest time, I automatically attributed this to Joshua, but as I have been waiting on the Lord for understanding, I have come to realize that there is far more contained within the faith of the walls falling down. Today we are not standing before a particular person, but a body of believers who stepped into unity with all the generations. There is momentum to be received within this group of people that marched around this city for seven days. Come let us step into the momentum of the past to carry it into our present and equip us for the future.

Now Faith

If you have not read about the beginning of the leadership of Joshua, I would like to encourage you to take a detour into Joshua chapters 1-6 and watch the handing of the leadership of Moses to Joshua his assistant. The baton is being handed to another as it was from Abraham to Isaac, to Jacob to Joseph, and then picked up by Moses, and finally, Joshua. Moses led the children of Israel to the edge of the Promised Land and now Joshua would lead them into it. Their first obstacle was Jericho. What is your Jericho today? This was a city completely protected by walls and seemingly invincible.

What would it have been like to walk around a city for six days in a row? I wonder if they were excited to face those high walls each day. I wonder if to some it felt silly to just walk around the city and be quiet. The people on the inside of the city would have been watching and wondering and maybe even yelling at them and making fun of them. Day after day, they got up and as one unit; they obeyed and did what the Lord had given them to do. Does this make sense to you? Has the Lord asked you to do things that seemed ridiculous and so you chose not to do them? What do you need from this body of believers today?

As I have focused on this verse and situation, I saw that each day the walls would not have looked as big as the day before. The mocking would not have been as insulting as in the beginning and each day something grew inside of them. They would have been thinking about what God had asked them to do and they were doing it. They were instructed to be silent, so they only had their thoughts. I see this connected to Hebrews 11:6, "But without faith it is impossible to please

Him, for he who comes to God must believe that He is, and that He is a rewarder of those who diligently seek Him." As they marched around that city, they were pleasing Him and learning personally that He is and that He is a rewarder of those who diligently seek Him. I believe they were thinking of the provision, of the stories they were told of the exodus from Egypt, the parting of the Red Sea, and everything that the generations before them had handed down to them. They were a part Walls of Jericho Fell of that and walking out another great testimony. I believe that all of heaven was walking around those walls day after day with them, reminding them of the faithfulness of their God.

By the time it got to the seventh day, their faith would have been stronger than ever before and when they yelled at those walls all of heaven was yelling with them. Did they close their eyes and yell with all that was within them? They released faith and God moved on their behalf. Their reward was witnessed with their very eyes. They connected into the momentum of heaven and we can too. If you go back and look at the order of each person in Hebrews 11, you can see the momentum that was building and the moving of God's hand on the behalf of those who sought Him and believed in Him. Jericho to each of us represents the situations that seem impossible to get through. What do you need the Lord to move out of the way for you to move forward into your Promised Land? I believe that all of heaven wants to release before you what got released that seventh day. Are you ready to receive? I believe that before each of us as leaders there is an impartation to lead as Joshua did, to lead people into breakthrough personally. What do you need today?

Prayer for Impartation of Faith

Lord Jesus, I need an impartation of the faith that is available from Joshua and all of the Israelites that marched around that city for seven days believing that You were going to do what You said that You were going to do. Give me the faith to face my own impossible obstacles with You. Impart in me the obedience that they walked in. I need their faith and the momentum of the generations that had gone before them. Please empower me as I look at walls before me, and as I connect to their faith may these walls fall down. Impart in me their courage, obedience, and what was happening within them as they got up each day and faced their fears and weaknesses with You. I ask for an impartation of the generational faith of strength and courage that Joshua led with and exhibited as he led that brought unity and victory. Thank You so much for all that You are going to do with me. I ask and receive all of this known and unknown faith in the name of Jesus, amen!

Rahab

"By faith the harlot Rahab did not perish with those who did not believe, when she had received the spies with peace" (Heb. 11:31).

Rahab the harlot. How would you like that for a title? Who was this harlot Rahab and why is she within this list? What do we need from her faith?

The harlot Rahab shows up out of nowhere in Joshua chapter 2, when the spies that Joshua sent into Jericho lodged at her home. Why did they choose her home? This moment in time is pivotal for her. She recognizes who these spies are, allows them to come into her home, hides them from the king of Jericho, and asks for them to spare her when they come back to destroy the city. What would cause a harlot to do such a thing? We just read in the previous chapter about Joshua and the Israelites circling the city for seven days and the harlot Rahab was inside the city waiting to be rescued. She had heard of their God and believed. She saw their God as her hope for a new life and out of the name she had come to wear. Rahab wanted to be a part of what the Lord their

God was doing and she risked everything to walk in that. They saved her and her family, she walked in what she had longed for. If you read through the genealogy of Jesus, you will see her name appear not as a harlot but as Rahab the mother of Boaz. She was grafted in and got a new life. Is this what you desire from Rahab?

As I stand before Rahab today, I look into her eyes and I see a fresh start available. I no longer see pain and shame, but purpose and destiny. Rahab went from being a part of a community that was not looked upon as respectful and she was used and felt unworthy, to being a part of a community who served God. She heard the stories about the hope of God. She took a chance, found Him, and everything changed. There are people around us all the time wherever we are that feel as Rahab felt in that life in the city. Do we notice them? Have they even heard of our God, and what He can do for them? What do you need from the life and faith of Rahab?

Rahab was a harlot, or prostitute. The word prostitute is normally used for someone who takes money for using their body or abilities in ways they should not. We know the obvious meaning of the word, but the underlying truth reveals something different. Do we sell our talents to an unworthy cause? Do we know we are doing that? When we sell our talents to an unworthy purpose, it creates within us a place that feels unworthy. She had a place within her that somehow believed in God with everything working against her.

I see Rahab pleasing God even with just a small amount of faith. If we look at Hebrews 11:6 again, "But without faith it is impossible to please Him, for he who comes to God must believe that He is, and that He is a rewarder of those who diligently seek Him." This does not say how Rahab much faith we need to have, nor does it qualify who is included in this. Rahab had a small amount of faith from hearing stories of what God had done for the Israelites and began to believe that He is, and that He is a rewarder of those who diligently seek Him. The stories produced faith the size of a mustard seed and everything changed for her. I see our testimonies releasing potential for others to receive. Do you need to make a total change of direction in your life?

The faith of Rahab today offers fresh hope, new direction, and broken bondages. It can graft you into a destiny that was not originally intended for you, to be part of a generation that follows after and serves God. Do you need any of these things in your life?

Prayer for Impartation of Faith

Lord Jesus, thank You for the life and faith of Rahab. Thank You for showing me that I, too, can take the amount of faith I have and place it in You and You can change everything in my life. Forgive me for selling my talents to unworthy causes. I forgive myself and ask that You please begin working and changing my thoughts, my words, my actions, and my life. I need the faith of Rahab and all that is contained within it, seen and unseen. May I hear as she heard and have the courage that she had to risk it all for a life with You. May

Now Faith

I notice those around me who also have the ears and eyes of Rahab. For those that feel lost and are reaching out for that small place of hope for a new life and future. Impart in me the faith of Rahab and may it influence how I see myself, see You, and see others. Thank You for all that I am receiving. May this moment in time begin to stir new life and hope in me. Impart the faith of Rahab from every direction and every perspective in me now in the name of Jesus, amen!

And What More Shall I Say?

At this point in the chapter, each of the "by faith" statements have all stopped, and yet, the courage of more individuals and what they endured continues in verses 32-38.

32 And what more shall I say? For the time would fail me to tell of Gideon and Barak and Samson and Jephthah, also of David and Samuel and the prophets:

33 who through faith subdued kingdoms, worked righteousness, obtained promises, stopped the mouths of lions,

34 quenched the violence of fire, escaped the edge of the sword, out of weakness were made strong, became valiant in battle, turned to flight the armies of the aliens.

35 Women received their dead raised to life again. Others were tortured, not accepting deliverance, that they might obtain a better resurrection.

36 Still others had trial of mockings and scourgings, yes, and of chains and imprisonment.

37 They were stoned, they were sawn in two, were tempted, were slain with the sword. They wandered about in sheepskins and goatskins, being destitute, afflicted, tormented—

38 of whom the world was not worthy. They wandered in deserts and mountains, in dens and caves of the earth.

Every time I read the next seven verses that follow Rahab, I experience their courage and faith. I get to step into the faith that created in them an ability to go against all odds and keep their eyes on God. On days when I am a bit discouraged and wondering what I am doing on this planet I read Hebrews 11. When I am in this mindset, I read quickly past Abel, Enoch, Noah, Abraham, Sarah, Moses, Jericho, and Rahab and begin to feel something shift in my faith as I enter into these verses. By the time I get to verse 40, the heaviness that I entered with in verse 1 is gone and I am ready to start my day.

Hebrews chapter 11 is a faith tunnel that is necessary for all the followers of Jesus Christ. May you read this chapter in Hebrews many times and share it with others.

This Is My Prayer for You

Lord Jesus, I lift up the person reading these words right now and I ask that they would personally encounter You in ways that they never even imagined. May their faith be increased and their perspective of their life and circumstances be more in line with how You see them. I pray that the faith of each of these men and women would truly remain imparted within them and that they would have a noticeable revelation of how it is changing within them. May this faith that they have received be tangible in some way. I pray for increased visions, dreams, revelation, faith, hope, love, and the mentality that all things are possible. I pray that You will expand their heart and mind to Your ways and Your thinking. I ask for increased discernment and wisdom to walk in all that they have received. May the impartations from this book be protected, nurtured, and allowed to grow and expand who they are. I pray that this impartation of faith will awaken them to the depth of Your Word and that each day the truth of Your Word and their walk with You will grow exceedingly and abundantly above all that they could ever ask or think. I pray that their name will follow one of the "by faith" statements and that their life, thinking process, and faith will never be the same again. Bless them in all that they do for the rest of their life. Bless the generations that will follow them or that they have influence with. Thank You for the impartation of faith that pleases You. I ask all of this in the name of Jesus, amen!

"And all these, having obtained a good testimony through faith, did not receive the promise, God having provided something better for us, that they should not be made perfect apart from us" (Hebrews 11:39-40).

You are within the word "us."

Reflection of Faith

From each of the people highlighted in this book, you were presented with an opportunity to receive an impartation of their faith. I believe throughout your life there will be different parts of their faith you need specifically for where the Lord has you in your journey. Take time and reflect on the faith that you have received.

You have now received…

The able heart of Abel

The intimate walk of Enoch

The persevering and determined faith of Noah

The obedient daily faith of Abraham

The conception of strength from Sarah

These all died in faith

Testing of faith

The perspective of generational faith

Destiny faith and the courage of Moses

The breakthrough faith to remove barriers

The awareness faith of Rahab

What more shall I say? (Your faith)

You have now received faith that pleases God.

Faith that has a greater capacity to see that He is and that He is a rewarder of those who diligently seek Him.

The substance of our hope is Him…

The evidence is Him…

We are complete in Him…

About the Author

Cheryl Stasinowsky is a speaker and writer of passion and transparency. Her desire is for others to see Jesus in everything they walk through; growing a new passion for His Word and its relevance for them. Please contact her to make arrangements for your future events, retreats, church services, meetings, and conferences. She would love to meet you!

Contact Cheryl if you would like to plan a faith impartation weekend so all that is in this book can be released.

www.wordscribeministries.com
www.hishiddentreasure.blogspot.com
cheryl@wordscribeministries.com
Connect with Cheryl on Facebook
and Twitter @histreasures too!

What others are saying:

"Cheryl Stasinowsky is a treasure. Cheryl is a special artist that paints her teachings in faith constructionism, and as such, she passionately extracts the blueprints from the foundation of the Word and then builds that foundation into the details of everyday practical life. Her books and teachings are a life guide, and her speaking appearances are personal. She opens herself to each person she is teaching, and lays out in honesty her own personal experiences of the presence of God within the joys and pains of everyday life."

More Titles by Cheryl Stasinowsky

His Hidden Treasures
ISBN: 978-0-6158979-9-8

There is an unknown treasure sitting on your night stand, bookshelf or coffee table. It is full of keys that will unlock your destiny, vision and purpose. They are yours for the taking. Join Cheryl on this journey as she uncovers valuable secrets found in the Bible. Through her own brokenness and surrender, the author will inspire you to embark on your own journey of searching for the timeless and endless treasures in the Word of God. As you dig deeper, each hidden treasure will leave you desperate for more of God's Word.

Deeper Relevance
ISBN: 978-0-6159069-9-7

Cheryl set out to write a daily encouraging word on her social networks, not realizing that her pursuit for a deeper understanding of God's Word would blossom into a full devotional. Grab your Bible, along with this book, and get ready to discover kingdom nuggets that will enrich your walk and relationship with Jesus. His Word truly sustains us every day!

More Titles by Cheryl Stasinowsky

Now Faith in Spanish (Es Pues, La Fe)
ISBN: 978-0-615899-67-1

Es Pues, La Fe es un encuentro, cara a cara, con los hombres y mujeres de Hebreos 11 quienes tuvieron la fe que agradó a Dios y que movió montañas. Cada capítulo toma un paso adentro de sus vidas, echa un vistazo a su forma de ser, encuentra partes vitales del ADN de su fe, y después suple una oración para la impartición de esa fe.

Private Moments With God
ISBN: 978-0-6159103-7-6

Life as we individually know it ... Each of us has a past that is influencing how we see our present. We walk through our day with all of the pressures and demands of life with a past, in the present, and also with a hope for a future. I, too, journey this thing called life. Through it all, I have come to value to the highest degree the first moments of my early mornings when the house is quiet, it is still dark outside, my coffee is freshly brewed, my iPod is playing worship music in my ears, and I open the Word of God for my nourishment and encouragement for the day. These are those moments ...

More Titles by Cheryl Stasinowsky

Given to Forgive
ISBN: 978-0-692306-60-4

Are you tired of wrestling with regret, guilt, anger, resentment, bitterness, and impatience? Did you know that all of these are symptoms of unforgiveness? I did not like to forgive and always thought that the other person had to come to me first to apologize. I held onto unforgiveness for years. Eight years ago, I started forgiving people, situations, and choices I had made. I hand you my journey of choosing to be given to forgive every day...

Given to Love
ISBN: 978-0-692485-51-4

It is not going to be what you think it is going to be. This is not a book on love as the world sees and shows love. This is a book on my journey through discovering how to love from His word working in and through me. I have purposed to try to put on His word and live love. I am still learning, but what I have learned, I give. It has been tested and tried and has hurt a lot. I have submitted to Him in difficult situations and have chosen

More Titles by Cheryl Stasinowsky

Given to Prayer
ISBN: 978-0-692629-68-0

This is not a book on formulas to pray better. This is a book filled with my own personal journey in learning how He communicates with me. I share thoughts, struggles, victories, and defeats. I do not profess to have prayer all figured out. I think it is a life-long discovery for each individual.

Coming soon:

GIVEN TO CHANGE

GIVEN TO LISTEN

All of Cheryl's books are available in
eBook and print versions on Amazon and Barnes & Noble.

www.ingramcontent.com/pod-product-compliance
Lightning Source LLC
Chambersburg PA
CBHW071312040426
42444CB00009B/1987